50 Cozy Soups for Cold Nights

By: Kelly Johnson

Table of Contents

- Classic Tomato Soup with Grilled Cheese
- Creamy Potato Leek Soup
- Chicken and Wild Rice Soup
- Beef and Barley Soup
- Butternut Squash Soup
- Roasted Cauliflower Soup
- French Onion Soup
- Chicken Tortilla Soup
- Lentil and Vegetable Soup
- Clam Chowder
- Split Pea Soup with Ham
- Creamy Broccoli Cheddar Soup
- Minestrone Soup
- Pumpkin Soup with Coconut Milk
- Sweet Potato and Carrot Soup
- White Bean and Kale Soup
- Tomato Basil Soup
- Chicken and Dumpling Soup
- Beef Stew Soup
- Egg Drop Soup
- Mushroom and Barley Soup
- Cabbage and Sausage Soup
- Sweet Corn and Chicken Soup
- Spicy Sausage and Bean Soup
- Broccoli and Cheddar Soup
- Zucchini and Potato Soup
- Chicken Noodle Soup
- Roasted Tomato Soup with Parmesan
- Spicy Lentil Soup
- Turkey and Rice Soup
- Roasted Garlic and Potato Soup
- Potato Bacon Soup
- Chicken and Corn Chowder
- Carrot Ginger Soup
- Shrimp and Sausage Gumbo

- Creamy Spinach and Artichoke Soup
- Cucumber and Yogurt Soup
- Chicken and Sweet Potato Soup
- Black Bean Soup
- Italian Wedding Soup
- Sausage and Potato Soup
- Carrot and Leek Soup
- Pear and Parsnip Soup
- Roasted Red Pepper Soup
- Kale and White Bean Soup
- Roasted Beet and Feta Soup
- Spicy Pumpkin Soup
- Mexican Chicken Soup
- Chickpea and Spinach Soup
- Papprika Chicken Soup

Classic Tomato Soup with Grilled Cheese

Ingredients:

- **For the Tomato Soup:**
    - 2 tbsp olive oil
    - 1 onion, chopped
    - 2 garlic cloves, minced
    - 2 cans (14.5 oz each) diced tomatoes
    - 1 cup vegetable broth
    - 1/2 tsp dried basil
    - 1/4 tsp sugar
    - Salt and pepper to taste
    - 1/2 cup heavy cream (optional)
- **For the Grilled Cheese:**
    - 4 slices of bread
    - 4 tbsp butter
    - 4 slices cheddar cheese

Instructions:

1. **For the Soup:**
    - Heat olive oil in a large pot over medium heat. Add the onion and garlic and sauté until softened, about 5 minutes.
    - Add the diced tomatoes, vegetable broth, basil, sugar, salt, and pepper. Bring to a boil, then reduce heat and simmer for 15-20 minutes.
    - Blend the soup using an immersion blender or transfer to a regular blender, blending until smooth. Stir in the heavy cream, if using.
2. **For the Grilled Cheese:**
    - Butter each slice of bread on one side. Place a slice of cheese between two pieces of bread, buttered sides out.
    - Cook in a skillet over medium heat for 3-4 minutes per side, until golden brown and the cheese is melted.
3. Serve the soup with a grilled cheese sandwich on the side. Enjoy!

Creamy Potato Leek Soup

Ingredients:

- 2 tbsp butter
- 2 leeks, cleaned and chopped
- 3 medium potatoes, peeled and diced
- 4 cups vegetable broth
- 1 cup heavy cream
- Salt and pepper to taste
- Fresh parsley for garnish

Instructions:

1. In a large pot, melt butter over medium heat. Add the leeks and sauté until softened, about 5 minutes.
2. Add the potatoes and vegetable broth. Bring to a boil, then reduce heat and simmer for 20 minutes or until the potatoes are tender.
3. Using an immersion blender, puree the soup until smooth. Stir in the heavy cream and season with salt and pepper.
4. Garnish with fresh parsley and serve.

Chicken and Wild Rice Soup

Ingredients:

- 1 tbsp olive oil
- 1 onion, chopped
- 2 carrots, diced
- 2 celery stalks, diced
- 3 garlic cloves, minced
- 1 cup wild rice, rinsed
- 6 cups chicken broth
- 2 cups cooked chicken, shredded
- 1 tsp dried thyme
- 1/2 cup heavy cream
- Salt and pepper to taste

Instructions:

1. Heat olive oil in a large pot over medium heat. Add the onion, carrots, celery, and garlic. Cook until softened, about 5 minutes.
2. Stir in the wild rice, chicken broth, cooked chicken, thyme, salt, and pepper. Bring to a boil, then reduce heat and simmer for 25-30 minutes, until the rice is tender.
3. Stir in the heavy cream and adjust seasoning as needed. Serve warm.

Beef and Barley Soup

Ingredients:

- 1 lb beef stew meat, cubed
- 2 tbsp olive oil
- 1 onion, chopped
- 2 carrots, sliced
- 2 celery stalks, chopped
- 2 garlic cloves, minced
- 6 cups beef broth
- 1 cup pearl barley
- 1 tsp dried thyme
- Salt and pepper to taste
- Fresh parsley for garnish

Instructions:

1. Heat olive oil in a large pot over medium heat. Brown the beef stew meat on all sides, then remove and set aside.
2. In the same pot, sauté the onion, carrots, celery, and garlic for 5 minutes, until softened.
3. Add the beef broth, pearl barley, thyme, salt, and pepper. Bring to a boil, then reduce heat and simmer for 45 minutes or until the barley and beef are tender.
4. Garnish with fresh parsley and serve.

Butternut Squash Soup

Ingredients:

- 2 tbsp olive oil
- 1 onion, chopped
- 1 butternut squash, peeled and diced
- 2 carrots, peeled and diced
- 4 cups vegetable broth
- 1/2 tsp ground cinnamon
- Salt and pepper to taste
- 1/2 cup heavy cream (optional)

Instructions:

1. Heat olive oil in a large pot over medium heat. Add the onion and sauté for 5 minutes until softened.
2. Add the butternut squash, carrots, vegetable broth, cinnamon, salt, and pepper. Bring to a boil, then reduce heat and simmer for 25-30 minutes, or until the vegetables are tender.
3. Blend the soup using an immersion blender or transfer to a regular blender until smooth. Stir in the heavy cream, if desired.
4. Serve warm.

Roasted Cauliflower Soup

Ingredients:

- 1 medium head of cauliflower, cut into florets
- 2 tbsp olive oil
- Salt and pepper to taste
- 1 onion, chopped
- 2 garlic cloves, minced
- 4 cups vegetable broth
- 1/2 cup heavy cream (optional)
- Fresh thyme for garnish

Instructions:

1. Preheat the oven to 400°F (200°C). Toss the cauliflower florets with olive oil, salt, and pepper, then spread on a baking sheet. Roast for 20-25 minutes, or until golden and tender.
2. In a large pot, sauté the onion and garlic for 5 minutes, until softened.
3. Add the roasted cauliflower and vegetable broth to the pot. Bring to a boil, then reduce heat and simmer for 10 minutes.
4. Use an immersion blender to puree the soup until smooth. Stir in the heavy cream, if desired.
5. Garnish with fresh thyme and serve.

French Onion Soup

Ingredients:

- 2 tbsp butter
- 4 large onions, thinly sliced
- 2 garlic cloves, minced
- 1 tbsp fresh thyme, chopped
- 6 cups beef broth
- 1 cup dry white wine
- 1 bay leaf
- Salt and pepper to taste
- 4 slices French bread
- 1 1/2 cups shredded Gruyère cheese

Instructions:

1. In a large pot, melt butter over medium heat. Add the onions and cook, stirring occasionally, for 25-30 minutes, until the onions are caramelized.
2. Add the garlic, thyme, beef broth, wine, bay leaf, salt, and pepper. Bring to a boil, then reduce heat and simmer for 20 minutes.
3. Meanwhile, toast the French bread slices in the oven until crispy.
4. Ladle the soup into oven-safe bowls, top with a slice of toasted bread, and sprinkle with Gruyère cheese.
5. Place the bowls under the broiler for 2-3 minutes, until the cheese is melted and bubbly. Serve warm.

Chicken Tortilla Soup

Ingredients:

- 2 tbsp olive oil
- 1 onion, chopped
- 2 garlic cloves, minced
- 1 can (14.5 oz) diced tomatoes
- 4 cups chicken broth
- 2 cups cooked chicken, shredded
- 1 tsp chili powder
- 1/2 tsp cumin
- 1/4 tsp cayenne pepper (optional)
- Salt and pepper to taste
- 1 cup tortilla chips, crushed
- 1/2 cup shredded cheddar cheese
- 1/2 cup sour cream
- Fresh cilantro for garnish

Instructions:

1. Heat olive oil in a large pot over medium heat. Add the onion and garlic and sauté until softened, about 5 minutes.
2. Stir in the diced tomatoes, chicken broth, shredded chicken, chili powder, cumin, cayenne pepper, salt, and pepper. Bring to a boil, then reduce heat and simmer for 15-20 minutes.
3. Stir in the crushed tortilla chips and cook for another 5 minutes.
4. Ladle the soup into bowls and top with shredded cheese, sour cream, and fresh cilantro. Serve immediately.

Lentil and Vegetable Soup

Ingredients:

- 2 tbsp olive oil
- 1 onion, chopped
- 2 carrots, diced
- 2 celery stalks, diced
- 2 garlic cloves, minced
- 1 cup dried lentils, rinsed
- 6 cups vegetable broth
- 1 can (14.5 oz) diced tomatoes
- 1 tsp dried thyme
- 1/2 tsp ground cumin
- Salt and pepper to taste
- Fresh parsley for garnish

Instructions:

1. Heat olive oil in a large pot over medium heat. Add the onion, carrots, celery, and garlic and sauté for 5 minutes.
2. Add the lentils, vegetable broth, diced tomatoes, thyme, cumin, salt, and pepper. Bring to a boil, then reduce heat and simmer for 30-40 minutes, until the lentils are tender.
3. Garnish with fresh parsley and serve warm.

Clam Chowder

Ingredients:

- 2 tbsp butter
- 1 onion, chopped
- 2 celery stalks, chopped
- 2 garlic cloves, minced
- 4 large potatoes, peeled and diced
- 2 cups clam juice
- 1 can (14.5 oz) chopped clams, drained
- 1 1/2 cups heavy cream
- Salt and pepper to taste
- Fresh parsley for garnish

Instructions:

1. In a large pot, melt butter over medium heat. Add the onion, celery, and garlic, and cook until softened, about 5 minutes.
2. Add the diced potatoes, clam juice, and enough water to cover the potatoes. Bring to a boil, then reduce heat and simmer for 15-20 minutes until the potatoes are tender.
3. Stir in the clams and heavy cream. Season with salt and pepper to taste, and simmer for 5 minutes.
4. Garnish with fresh parsley and serve warm.

Split Pea Soup with Ham

Ingredients:

- 1 tbsp olive oil
- 1 onion, chopped
- 2 carrots, diced
- 2 celery stalks, diced
- 2 garlic cloves, minced
- 2 cups dried split peas, rinsed
- 6 cups vegetable or chicken broth
- 1 tsp dried thyme
- 1 bay leaf
- 2 cups cooked ham, diced
- Salt and pepper to taste

Instructions:

1. Heat olive oil in a large pot over medium heat. Add the onion, carrots, celery, and garlic, and cook until softened, about 5 minutes.
2. Add the split peas, broth, thyme, bay leaf, ham, salt, and pepper. Bring to a boil, then reduce heat and simmer for 45 minutes to 1 hour, or until the peas are tender and the soup thickens.
3. Remove the bay leaf, adjust seasoning, and serve warm.

Creamy Broccoli Cheddar Soup

Ingredients:

- 2 tbsp butter
- 1 onion, chopped
- 3 cups broccoli florets
- 2 cups vegetable broth
- 1 cup milk
- 1 1/2 cups shredded sharp cheddar cheese
- Salt and pepper to taste
- 1 tbsp flour (optional, for thickening)

Instructions:

1. In a large pot, melt butter over medium heat. Add the onion and cook until softened, about 5 minutes.
2. Add the broccoli and vegetable broth. Bring to a boil, then reduce heat and simmer for 15 minutes or until the broccoli is tender.
3. Use an immersion blender to blend the soup until smooth (or leave it chunky if preferred). Stir in the milk and cheese, and season with salt and pepper.
4. If you want a thicker soup, mix the flour with a little water to form a slurry, then stir into the soup and simmer for a few more minutes. Serve warm.

Minestrone Soup

Ingredients:

- 2 tbsp olive oil
- 1 onion, chopped
- 2 carrots, diced
- 2 celery stalks, diced
- 2 garlic cloves, minced
- 1 zucchini, diced
- 1 cup green beans, chopped
- 1 can (14.5 oz) diced tomatoes
- 4 cups vegetable broth
- 1 can (15 oz) kidney beans, drained and rinsed
- 1 cup pasta (small shells or ditalini)
- 1 tsp dried oregano
- Salt and pepper to taste
- Fresh basil for garnish

Instructions:

1. Heat olive oil in a large pot over medium heat. Add the onion, carrots, celery, and garlic, and cook until softened, about 5 minutes.
2. Add the zucchini, green beans, diced tomatoes, vegetable broth, kidney beans, pasta, oregano, salt, and pepper. Bring to a boil, then reduce heat and simmer for 20 minutes, until the pasta is cooked and the vegetables are tender.
3. Garnish with fresh basil and serve warm.

Pumpkin Soup with Coconut Milk

Ingredients:

- 2 tbsp olive oil
- 1 onion, chopped
- 2 garlic cloves, minced
- 1 can (15 oz) pumpkin puree
- 4 cups vegetable broth
- 1 can (14 oz) coconut milk
- 1 tsp ground cinnamon
- 1/2 tsp ground nutmeg
- Salt and pepper to taste
- Fresh parsley for garnish

Instructions:

1. Heat olive oil in a large pot over medium heat. Add the onion and garlic, and sauté until softened, about 5 minutes.
2. Stir in the pumpkin puree, vegetable broth, coconut milk, cinnamon, nutmeg, salt, and pepper. Bring to a boil, then reduce heat and simmer for 10-15 minutes.
3. Use an immersion blender to blend the soup until smooth. Adjust seasoning to taste.
4. Garnish with fresh parsley and serve warm.

Sweet Potato and Carrot Soup

Ingredients:

- 2 tbsp olive oil
- 1 onion, chopped
- 2 garlic cloves, minced
- 2 large sweet potatoes, peeled and diced
- 4 carrots, peeled and diced
- 4 cups vegetable broth
- 1 tsp ground cumin
- Salt and pepper to taste
- Fresh cilantro for garnish

Instructions:

1. Heat olive oil in a large pot over medium heat. Add the onion and garlic, and cook until softened, about 5 minutes.
2. Add the sweet potatoes, carrots, vegetable broth, cumin, salt, and pepper. Bring to a boil, then reduce heat and simmer for 25-30 minutes, until the vegetables are tender.
3. Use an immersion blender to blend the soup until smooth. Adjust seasoning to taste.
4. Garnish with fresh cilantro and serve warm.

White Bean and Kale Soup

Ingredients:

- 2 tbsp olive oil
- 1 onion, chopped
- 2 garlic cloves, minced
- 1 can (15 oz) white beans, drained and rinsed
- 4 cups vegetable broth
- 2 cups kale, chopped
- 1 tsp dried thyme
- Salt and pepper to taste
- 1 tbsp lemon juice

Instructions:

1. Heat olive oil in a large pot over medium heat. Add the onion and garlic, and cook until softened, about 5 minutes.
2. Add the white beans, vegetable broth, kale, thyme, salt, and pepper. Bring to a boil, then reduce heat and simmer for 15-20 minutes.
3. Stir in the lemon juice and adjust seasoning to taste.
4. Serve warm.

Tomato Basil Soup

Ingredients:

- 2 tbsp olive oil
- 1 onion, chopped
- 2 garlic cloves, minced
- 2 cans (14.5 oz each) diced tomatoes
- 4 cups vegetable broth
- 1 tsp dried basil
- Salt and pepper to taste
- 1/2 cup heavy cream (optional)
- Fresh basil for garnish

Instructions:

1. Heat olive oil in a large pot over medium heat. Add the onion and garlic, and sauté until softened, about 5 minutes.
2. Add the diced tomatoes, vegetable broth, basil, salt, and pepper. Bring to a boil, then reduce heat and simmer for 15-20 minutes.
3. Use an immersion blender to blend the soup until smooth. Stir in the heavy cream if desired.
4. Garnish with fresh basil and serve warm.

Chicken and Dumpling Soup

Ingredients:

- 2 tbsp butter
- 1 onion, chopped
- 2 carrots, diced
- 2 celery stalks, diced
- 2 garlic cloves, minced
- 6 cups chicken broth
- 2 cups cooked chicken, shredded
- 1 tsp dried thyme
- Salt and pepper to taste
- **For the Dumplings:**
    - 1 cup flour
    - 1 1/2 tsp baking powder
    - 1/2 tsp salt
    - 1/2 tsp dried thyme
    - 3/4 cup milk
    - 2 tbsp butter, melted

Instructions:

1. In a large pot, melt butter over medium heat. Add the onion, carrots, celery, and garlic, and cook until softened, about 5 minutes.
2. Add the chicken broth, cooked chicken, thyme, salt, and pepper. Bring to a boil, then reduce heat and simmer for 10 minutes.
3. **For the Dumplings:** In a bowl, mix the flour, baking powder, salt, and thyme. Stir in the milk and melted butter until just combined.
4. Drop spoonfuls of the dumpling batter into the simmering soup. Cover and cook for 15-20 minutes, until the dumplings are cooked through.
5. Serve warm.

Beef Stew Soup

Ingredients:

- 1 lb beef stew meat, cubed
- 2 tbsp olive oil
- 1 onion, chopped
- 2 carrots, sliced
- 2 potatoes, peeled and diced
- 2 garlic cloves, minced
- 4 cups beef broth
- 1 tsp dried thyme
- 1 bay leaf
- Salt and pepper to taste

Instructions:

1. Heat olive oil in a large pot over medium heat. Brown the beef stew meat on all sides, then remove and set aside.
2. In the same pot, sauté the onion, carrots, potatoes, and garlic for 5 minutes.
3. Add the beef broth, thyme, bay leaf, salt, and pepper. Bring to a boil, then reduce heat and simmer for 1 hour, or until the beef is tender.
4. Remove the bay leaf and serve warm.

Egg Drop Soup

Ingredients:

- 4 cups chicken broth
- 2 large eggs, lightly beaten
- 1 tbsp cornstarch (optional for thicker soup)
- 1/4 tsp white pepper
- 1 tbsp soy sauce
- 2 green onions, chopped (for garnish)
- 1/2 tsp sesame oil (optional)

Instructions:

1. In a medium pot, bring the chicken broth to a boil over medium heat. If you want a thicker soup, dissolve the cornstarch in 2 tbsp of water and add it to the boiling broth.
2. Slowly pour the beaten eggs into the broth while stirring gently in one direction to create egg ribbons.
3. Add soy sauce, white pepper, and sesame oil (if using). Stir to combine.
4. Remove from heat and garnish with chopped green onions before serving.

Mushroom and Barley Soup

Ingredients:

- 2 tbsp olive oil
- 1 onion, chopped
- 2 garlic cloves, minced
- 2 cups mushrooms, sliced
- 1 cup barley
- 4 cups vegetable or chicken broth
- 2 carrots, diced
- 1 celery stalk, chopped
- 1 tsp dried thyme
- Salt and pepper to taste
- Fresh parsley for garnish

Instructions:

1. Heat olive oil in a large pot over medium heat. Add the onion and garlic, cooking until softened.
2. Stir in the mushrooms and cook for another 5 minutes, until they release their juices.
3. Add the barley, broth, carrots, celery, thyme, salt, and pepper. Bring to a boil, then reduce heat to a simmer.
4. Cook for 40-45 minutes, until the barley is tender.
5. Garnish with fresh parsley and serve warm.

Cabbage and Sausage Soup

Ingredients:

- 1 tbsp olive oil
- 1 onion, chopped
- 2 garlic cloves, minced
- 1 lb sausage (Italian or smoked), sliced
- 1 small head of cabbage, shredded
- 4 cups vegetable or chicken broth
- 1 can (14.5 oz) diced tomatoes
- 2 potatoes, peeled and diced
- 1 tsp dried thyme
- Salt and pepper to taste

Instructions:

1. Heat olive oil in a large pot over medium heat. Add the onion and garlic and cook until softened.
2. Add the sausage and cook until browned, breaking it apart as it cooks.
3. Stir in the cabbage, broth, diced tomatoes, potatoes, thyme, salt, and pepper. Bring to a boil.
4. Reduce heat and simmer for 30 minutes, until the potatoes are tender.
5. Serve warm.

Sweet Corn and Chicken Soup

Ingredients:

- 2 tbsp olive oil
- 1 onion, chopped
- 2 garlic cloves, minced
- 1 lb chicken breast, cooked and shredded
- 4 cups chicken broth
- 2 cups corn kernels (fresh, frozen, or canned)
- 1 tsp cumin
- 1/2 tsp chili powder
- Salt and pepper to taste
- Fresh cilantro for garnish

Instructions:

1. Heat olive oil in a large pot over medium heat. Add the onion and garlic, cooking until softened.
2. Add the shredded chicken, broth, corn, cumin, chili powder, salt, and pepper. Bring to a boil.
3. Reduce heat and simmer for 15-20 minutes.
4. Garnish with fresh cilantro and serve warm.

Spicy Sausage and Bean Soup

Ingredients:

- 1 tbsp olive oil
- 1 lb spicy sausage (Italian or chorizo), sliced
- 1 onion, chopped
- 2 garlic cloves, minced
- 1 can (15 oz) kidney beans, drained and rinsed
- 1 can (15 oz) diced tomatoes
- 4 cups vegetable or chicken broth
- 1 tsp smoked paprika
- 1/2 tsp red pepper flakes (optional)
- Salt and pepper to taste

Instructions:

1. Heat olive oil in a large pot over medium heat. Add the sausage and cook until browned.
2. Add the onion and garlic, and cook until softened.
3. Stir in the beans, tomatoes, broth, smoked paprika, red pepper flakes, salt, and pepper. Bring to a boil.
4. Reduce heat and simmer for 20 minutes.
5. Serve warm.

Broccoli and Cheddar Soup

Ingredients:

- 2 tbsp butter
- 1 onion, chopped
- 2 garlic cloves, minced
- 4 cups broccoli florets
- 4 cups vegetable or chicken broth
- 1 1/2 cups shredded cheddar cheese
- 1 cup milk
- Salt and pepper to taste

Instructions:

1. In a large pot, melt butter over medium heat. Add the onion and garlic, cooking until softened.
2. Add the broccoli and broth. Bring to a boil, then reduce heat and simmer for 15-20 minutes, until the broccoli is tender.
3. Use an immersion blender to blend the soup to your desired consistency (smooth or chunky).
4. Stir in the cheddar cheese and milk. Season with salt and pepper to taste.
5. Serve warm.

Zucchini and Potato Soup

Ingredients:

- 1 tbsp olive oil
- 1 onion, chopped
- 2 garlic cloves, minced
- 2 zucchinis, chopped
- 2 large potatoes, peeled and diced
- 4 cups vegetable or chicken broth
- Salt and pepper to taste
- Fresh thyme for garnish

Instructions:

1. Heat olive oil in a large pot over medium heat. Add the onion and garlic, cooking until softened.
2. Add the zucchinis, potatoes, and broth. Bring to a boil, then reduce heat and simmer for 25-30 minutes, until the potatoes are tender.
3. Use an immersion blender to blend the soup until smooth (optional).
4. Season with salt and pepper, and garnish with fresh thyme before serving.

Chicken Noodle Soup

Ingredients:

- 1 tbsp olive oil
- 1 onion, chopped
- 2 garlic cloves, minced
- 2 carrots, diced
- 2 celery stalks, chopped
- 4 cups chicken broth
- 2 cups cooked chicken, shredded
- 1 1/2 cups egg noodles
- Salt and pepper to taste
- Fresh parsley for garnish

Instructions:

1. Heat olive oil in a large pot over medium heat. Add the onion and garlic, cooking until softened.
2. Add the carrots, celery, and broth. Bring to a boil, then reduce heat and simmer for 10 minutes.
3. Stir in the shredded chicken and egg noodles, and cook until the noodles are tender, about 10 minutes.
4. Season with salt and pepper, and garnish with fresh parsley before serving.

Roasted Tomato Soup with Parmesan

Ingredients:

- 8 medium tomatoes, halved
- 1 tbsp olive oil
- 1 onion, chopped
- 2 garlic cloves, minced
- 4 cups vegetable or chicken broth
- Salt and pepper to taste
- 1 tsp dried basil
- 1/4 cup grated Parmesan cheese
- Fresh basil for garnish

Instructions:

1. Preheat the oven to 400°F (200°C). Place the halved tomatoes on a baking sheet and drizzle with olive oil. Roast for 25-30 minutes, until the tomatoes are soft and caramelized.
2. In a large pot, heat olive oil over medium heat. Add the chopped onion and garlic, cooking until softened (about 5 minutes).
3. Add the roasted tomatoes to the pot along with the broth, basil, salt, and pepper. Simmer for 15 minutes.
4. Use an immersion blender to blend the soup until smooth.
5. Stir in the grated Parmesan and serve garnished with fresh basil.

Spicy Lentil Soup

Ingredients:

- 1 tbsp olive oil
- 1 onion, chopped
- 2 garlic cloves, minced
- 2 carrots, diced
- 1 cup lentils (green or brown)
- 4 cups vegetable broth
- 1 can (14.5 oz) diced tomatoes
- 1 tsp cumin
- 1/2 tsp turmeric
- 1/2 tsp chili powder
- Salt and pepper to taste
- 1/4 tsp red pepper flakes (optional for extra spice)

Instructions:

1. Heat olive oil in a large pot over medium heat. Add the onion and garlic, cooking until softened.
2. Add the carrots and cook for another 5 minutes.
3. Stir in the lentils, broth, diced tomatoes, cumin, turmeric, chili powder, salt, pepper, and red pepper flakes (if using).
4. Bring to a boil, then reduce heat and simmer for 30-40 minutes, until the lentils are tender.
5. Serve warm.

Turkey and Rice Soup

Ingredients:

- 1 tbsp olive oil
- 1 onion, chopped
- 2 garlic cloves, minced
- 2 carrots, diced
- 2 celery stalks, chopped
- 4 cups turkey or chicken broth
- 2 cups cooked turkey (or chicken), shredded
- 1 cup cooked rice
- 1/2 tsp dried thyme
- Salt and pepper to taste

Instructions:

1. Heat olive oil in a large pot over medium heat. Add the onion and garlic, cooking until softened.
2. Add the carrots and celery, cooking for another 5 minutes.
3. Pour in the broth, shredded turkey, cooked rice, thyme, salt, and pepper. Bring to a boil.
4. Reduce heat and simmer for 15-20 minutes, until the vegetables are tender.
5. Serve warm.

Roasted Garlic and Potato Soup

Ingredients:

- 1 whole head garlic
- 1 tbsp olive oil
- 1 onion, chopped
- 4 cups vegetable or chicken broth
- 4 large potatoes, peeled and diced
- Salt and pepper to taste
- 1 cup heavy cream or milk (optional for creaminess)
- Fresh parsley for garnish

Instructions:

1. Preheat the oven to 400°F (200°C). Cut the top off the garlic head, drizzle with olive oil, and wrap in foil. Roast for 30 minutes, until soft.
2. In a large pot, heat olive oil over medium heat. Add the chopped onion and cook until softened.
3. Add the potatoes and broth to the pot, bringing it to a boil. Reduce heat and simmer for 20-25 minutes, until the potatoes are tender.
4. Squeeze the roasted garlic into the soup and blend with an immersion blender until smooth.
5. Stir in cream or milk (if using), season with salt and pepper, and garnish with fresh parsley before serving.

Potato Bacon Soup

Ingredients:

- 4 slices bacon, chopped
- 1 onion, chopped
- 2 garlic cloves, minced
- 4 cups vegetable or chicken broth
- 4 large potatoes, peeled and diced
- 1 cup heavy cream
- Salt and pepper to taste
- Fresh parsley for garnish

Instructions:

1. In a large pot, cook the bacon over medium heat until crispy. Remove and set aside, leaving some bacon fat in the pot.
2. Add the onion and garlic to the pot and cook until softened.
3. Add the potatoes and broth, bringing to a boil. Reduce heat and simmer for 20-25 minutes, until the potatoes are tender.
4. Stir in the heavy cream and cooked bacon. Blend the soup until smooth or leave some chunks for texture.
5. Season with salt and pepper and garnish with fresh parsley.

Chicken and Corn Chowder

Ingredients:

- 1 tbsp olive oil
- 1 onion, chopped
- 2 garlic cloves, minced
- 2 cups cooked chicken, shredded
- 2 cups corn kernels (fresh, frozen, or canned)
- 4 cups chicken broth
- 2 potatoes, peeled and diced
- 1 cup heavy cream or milk
- Salt and pepper to taste
- Fresh chives for garnish

Instructions:

1. Heat olive oil in a large pot over medium heat. Add the onion and garlic, cooking until softened.
2. Stir in the chicken, corn, broth, and potatoes. Bring to a boil, then reduce heat and simmer for 20 minutes, until the potatoes are tender.
3. Add the cream or milk and season with salt and pepper.
4. Serve garnished with fresh chives.

Carrot Ginger Soup

Ingredients:

- 1 tbsp olive oil
- 1 onion, chopped
- 3 garlic cloves, minced
- 4 cups carrots, peeled and chopped
- 1-inch piece of ginger, grated
- 4 cups vegetable or chicken broth
- Salt and pepper to taste
- 1 tbsp fresh lemon juice

Instructions:

1. Heat olive oil in a large pot over medium heat. Add the onion and garlic, cooking until softened.
2. Add the carrots and ginger, stirring for 2 minutes.
3. Pour in the broth and bring to a boil. Reduce heat and simmer for 20-25 minutes, until the carrots are tender.
4. Use an immersion blender to blend the soup until smooth. Season with salt, pepper, and lemon juice before serving.

Shrimp and Sausage Gumbo

Ingredients:

- 1 tbsp olive oil
- 1 sausage (Andouille or smoked), sliced
- 1 onion, chopped
- 2 garlic cloves, minced
- 1 bell pepper, chopped
- 2 cups shrimp, peeled and deveined
- 4 cups chicken broth
- 1 can (14.5 oz) diced tomatoes
- 1 tsp thyme
- 1/2 tsp paprika
- 1/2 tsp cayenne pepper (optional)
- Salt and pepper to taste
- 1 tbsp flour (optional for thickening)

Instructions:

1. Heat olive oil in a large pot over medium heat. Add the sausage and cook until browned.
2. Add the onion, garlic, and bell pepper, cooking until softened.
3. Stir in the shrimp, broth, tomatoes, thyme, paprika, cayenne, salt, and pepper.
4. If you want a thicker gumbo, make a roux by mixing flour with a little water, then stir it into the soup. Bring to a boil, then reduce heat and simmer for 15-20 minutes.
5. Serve warm.

Creamy Spinach and Artichoke Soup

Ingredients:

- 1 tbsp olive oil
- 1 onion, chopped
- 2 garlic cloves, minced
- 2 cups spinach, fresh or frozen
- 1 can (14 oz) artichoke hearts, drained and chopped
- 4 cups vegetable or chicken broth
- 1 cup heavy cream
- Salt and pepper to taste
- Fresh parsley for garnish

Instructions:

1. Heat olive oil in a large pot over medium heat. Add the onion and garlic, cooking until softened.
2. Stir in the spinach and artichokes, cooking until the spinach wilts.
3. Add the broth and bring to a boil. Reduce heat and simmer for 10 minutes.
4. Stir in the heavy cream and season with salt and pepper.
5. Use an immersion blender to blend the soup until smooth or leave it chunky. Garnish with fresh parsley before serving.

Cucumber and Yogurt Soup

Ingredients:

- 2 cucumbers, peeled and chopped
- 1 cup plain yogurt
- 1/2 cup sour cream (optional for extra creaminess)
- 1 tbsp olive oil
- 2 garlic cloves, minced
- 1 tbsp fresh dill, chopped
- 1 tbsp lemon juice
- Salt and pepper to taste

Instructions:

1. In a blender or food processor, combine the cucumbers, yogurt, sour cream (if using), olive oil, garlic, dill, and lemon juice.
2. Blend until smooth, adding a little water or extra yogurt if the soup is too thick.
3. Season with salt and pepper to taste.
4. Chill the soup in the refrigerator for at least 30 minutes before serving.
5. Serve garnished with additional dill or a drizzle of olive oil.

Chicken and Sweet Potato Soup

Ingredients:

- 1 tbsp olive oil
- 1 onion, chopped
- 2 garlic cloves, minced
- 2 medium sweet potatoes, peeled and diced
- 2 cups cooked chicken, shredded
- 4 cups chicken broth
- 1 tsp ground cumin
- Salt and pepper to taste
- Fresh cilantro for garnish (optional)

Instructions:

1. Heat olive oil in a large pot over medium heat. Add the onion and garlic, cooking until softened (about 5 minutes).
2. Add the sweet potatoes, cooked chicken, chicken broth, cumin, salt, and pepper to the pot. Bring to a boil.
3. Reduce heat and simmer for 20-25 minutes, until the sweet potatoes are tender.
4. Use an immersion blender to blend the soup to your desired consistency (smooth or chunky).
5. Serve garnished with fresh cilantro, if desired.

Black Bean Soup

Ingredients:

- 2 tbsp olive oil
- 1 onion, chopped
- 2 garlic cloves, minced
- 1 can (15 oz) black beans, drained and rinsed
- 4 cups vegetable or chicken broth
- 1 tsp cumin
- 1 tsp chili powder
- 1/2 tsp smoked paprika
- Salt and pepper to taste
- 1 lime, juiced
- Fresh cilantro for garnish

Instructions:

1. Heat olive oil in a large pot over medium heat. Add the onion and garlic, cooking until softened.
2. Stir in the black beans, broth, cumin, chili powder, smoked paprika, salt, and pepper. Bring to a boil.
3. Reduce heat and simmer for 15-20 minutes to allow the flavors to meld.
4. Use an immersion blender to blend the soup until smooth or leave it chunky.
5. Stir in the lime juice and serve garnished with fresh cilantro.

Italian Wedding Soup

Ingredients:

- 1 tbsp olive oil
- 1 onion, chopped
- 2 garlic cloves, minced
- 1/2 lb ground beef or turkey
- 1/4 cup grated Parmesan cheese
- 1/4 cup breadcrumbs
- 1 egg, beaten
- 6 cups chicken broth
- 1 cup cooked pasta (such as orzo or small shells)
- 4 cups fresh spinach, chopped
- Salt and pepper to taste

Instructions:

1. Heat olive oil in a large pot over medium heat. Add the onion and garlic, cooking until softened.
2. In a bowl, combine the ground meat, Parmesan cheese, breadcrumbs, and egg. Form the mixture into small meatballs (about 1 inch in diameter).
3. Add the meatballs to the pot and cook until browned on all sides.
4. Pour in the chicken broth and bring to a boil. Reduce heat and simmer for 15 minutes.
5. Add the cooked pasta and spinach to the pot and simmer for an additional 5-10 minutes, until the spinach is wilted.
6. Season with salt and pepper to taste and serve warm.

Sausage and Potato Soup

Ingredients:

- 1 tbsp olive oil
- 1 lb sausage (such as Italian or breakfast sausage), crumbled
- 1 onion, chopped
- 2 garlic cloves, minced
- 4 medium potatoes, peeled and diced
- 4 cups chicken broth
- 1 cup heavy cream
- 1/2 tsp thyme
- Salt and pepper to taste
- Fresh parsley for garnish

Instructions:

1. Heat olive oil in a large pot over medium heat. Add the sausage and cook, breaking it apart, until browned.
2. Add the onion and garlic, cooking until softened.
3. Add the potatoes, chicken broth, thyme, salt, and pepper. Bring to a boil.
4. Reduce heat and simmer for 20-25 minutes, until the potatoes are tender.
5. Stir in the heavy cream and cook for an additional 5 minutes.
6. Serve garnished with fresh parsley.

Carrot and Leek Soup

Ingredients:

- 1 tbsp olive oil
- 1 onion, chopped
- 2 leeks, cleaned and sliced
- 4 cups carrots, peeled and chopped
- 4 cups vegetable or chicken broth
- Salt and pepper to taste
- 1/2 tsp dried thyme
- 1 cup heavy cream or milk (optional for creaminess)

Instructions:

1. Heat olive oil in a large pot over medium heat. Add the onion and leeks, cooking until softened.
2. Stir in the carrots and cook for 5 minutes.
3. Add the broth, thyme, salt, and pepper. Bring to a boil.
4. Reduce heat and simmer for 20-25 minutes, until the carrots are tender.
5. Use an immersion blender to blend the soup until smooth. Add cream or milk if desired for a creamier texture.
6. Serve warm.

Pear and Parsnip Soup

Ingredients:

- 1 tbsp olive oil
- 1 onion, chopped
- 2 garlic cloves, minced
- 3 medium parsnips, peeled and chopped
- 3 pears, peeled and chopped
- 4 cups vegetable or chicken broth
- Salt and pepper to taste
- 1/2 tsp ground ginger
- Fresh parsley for garnish

Instructions:

1. Heat olive oil in a large pot over medium heat. Add the onion and garlic, cooking until softened.
2. Add the parsnips, pears, and ginger, and cook for 5 minutes.
3. Pour in the broth, salt, and pepper, and bring to a boil.
4. Reduce heat and simmer for 20-25 minutes, until the parsnips and pears are tender.
5. Use an immersion blender to blend the soup until smooth.
6. Serve garnished with fresh parsley.

Roasted Red Pepper Soup

Ingredients:

- 4 red bell peppers, halved and seeded
- 1 onion, chopped
- 2 garlic cloves, minced
- 2 cups vegetable broth
- 1 cup heavy cream (or coconut cream for dairy-free)
- 1 tbsp olive oil
- Salt and pepper to taste
- Fresh basil for garnish

Instructions:

1. Preheat the oven to 400°F (200°C). Place the red bell peppers on a baking sheet, skin-side up, and roast in the oven for 20-25 minutes, until the skins are charred and blistered.
2. Remove the peppers from the oven and cover them with a kitchen towel for 10 minutes. Once cooled, peel the skins off and chop the peppers.
3. Heat olive oil in a large pot over medium heat. Add the onion and garlic, cooking until softened, about 5 minutes.
4. Add the roasted red peppers and vegetable broth, bring to a boil, and simmer for 10 minutes.
5. Blend the soup until smooth using an immersion blender or in batches using a regular blender.
6. Stir in the heavy cream and season with salt and pepper to taste.
7. Serve garnished with fresh basil.

Kale and White Bean Soup

Ingredients:

- 1 tbsp olive oil
- 1 onion, chopped
- 2 garlic cloves, minced
- 1 can (15 oz) white beans, drained and rinsed
- 4 cups vegetable broth
- 2 cups kale, chopped
- 1 tsp dried thyme
- Salt and pepper to taste
- Juice of 1 lemon

Instructions:

1. Heat olive oil in a large pot over medium heat. Add the onion and garlic, cooking until softened.
2. Stir in the white beans, vegetable broth, thyme, salt, and pepper. Bring to a boil.
3. Reduce heat and simmer for 10-15 minutes to allow the flavors to meld.
4. Add the kale and simmer for an additional 5-7 minutes until the kale is wilted.
5. Stir in the lemon juice and adjust seasoning as needed.
6. Serve warm.

Roasted Beet and Feta Soup

Ingredients:

- 4 medium beets, peeled and chopped
- 1 onion, chopped
- 2 garlic cloves, minced
- 4 cups vegetable broth
- 1/2 cup crumbled feta cheese
- 1 tbsp olive oil
- Salt and pepper to taste
- Fresh dill for garnish

Instructions:

1. Preheat the oven to 400°F (200°C). Place the beets on a baking sheet, drizzle with olive oil, and season with salt and pepper. Roast for 30-40 minutes until tender.
2. Heat olive oil in a large pot over medium heat. Add the onion and garlic, cooking until softened.
3. Add the roasted beets and vegetable broth to the pot, and bring to a boil. Reduce heat and simmer for 10 minutes.
4. Use an immersion blender or regular blender to puree the soup until smooth.
5. Serve the soup topped with crumbled feta cheese and fresh dill.

Spicy Pumpkin Soup

Ingredients:

- 1 tbsp olive oil
- 1 onion, chopped
- 2 garlic cloves, minced
- 2 cups pumpkin puree
- 4 cups vegetable broth
- 1 tsp ground cumin
- 1 tsp smoked paprika
- 1/2 tsp cayenne pepper (adjust to taste)
- Salt and pepper to taste
- 1/2 cup coconut milk (optional for creaminess)
- Pumpkin seeds for garnish (optional)

Instructions:

1. Heat olive oil in a large pot over medium heat. Add the onion and garlic, cooking until softened.
2. Stir in the pumpkin puree, vegetable broth, cumin, smoked paprika, cayenne, salt, and pepper. Bring to a boil.
3. Reduce heat and simmer for 10-15 minutes to allow the flavors to meld.
4. Stir in the coconut milk, if using, and blend the soup until smooth using an immersion blender.
5. Serve the soup garnished with pumpkin seeds.

Mexican Chicken Soup

Ingredients:

- 1 tbsp olive oil
- 1 onion, chopped
- 2 garlic cloves, minced
- 1 can (15 oz) diced tomatoes
- 4 cups chicken broth
- 1 tsp chili powder
- 1 tsp cumin
- 2 cups cooked chicken, shredded
- 1 cup corn kernels (fresh, frozen, or canned)
- Salt and pepper to taste
- Fresh cilantro for garnish
- Lime wedges for serving

Instructions:

1. Heat olive oil in a large pot over medium heat. Add the onion and garlic, cooking until softened.
2. Stir in the diced tomatoes, chicken broth, chili powder, cumin, salt, and pepper. Bring to a boil.
3. Reduce heat and simmer for 15-20 minutes.
4. Add the shredded chicken and corn, and cook for another 5 minutes.
5. Serve the soup garnished with fresh cilantro and lime wedges.

Chickpea and Spinach Soup

Ingredients:

- 1 tbsp olive oil
- 1 onion, chopped
- 2 garlic cloves, minced
- 1 can (15 oz) chickpeas, drained and rinsed
- 4 cups vegetable broth
- 2 cups fresh spinach, chopped
- 1 tsp ground cumin
- Salt and pepper to taste
- 1 tbsp lemon juice
- Fresh parsley for garnish

Instructions:

1. Heat olive oil in a large pot over medium heat. Add the onion and garlic, cooking until softened.
2. Stir in the chickpeas, vegetable broth, cumin, salt, and pepper. Bring to a boil.
3. Reduce heat and simmer for 10-15 minutes.
4. Add the spinach and cook until wilted.
5. Stir in the lemon juice and adjust seasoning as needed.
6. Serve warm, garnished with fresh parsley.

Paprika Chicken Soup

Ingredients:

- 1 tbsp olive oil
- 1 onion, chopped
- 2 garlic cloves, minced
- 2 chicken breasts, cooked and shredded
- 4 cups chicken broth
- 1 tsp smoked paprika
- 1/2 tsp ground turmeric
- Salt and pepper to taste
- 1 cup diced potatoes
- 1/2 cup cream (optional for creaminess)
- Fresh parsley for garnish

Instructions:

1. Heat olive oil in a large pot over medium heat. Add the onion and garlic, cooking until softened.
2. Stir in the shredded chicken, chicken broth, smoked paprika, turmeric, salt, and pepper. Bring to a boil.
3. Add the diced potatoes and reduce heat. Simmer for 15-20 minutes until the potatoes are tender.
4. Stir in the cream if using, and cook for another 5 minutes.
5. Serve the soup garnished with fresh parsley.

www.ingramcontent.com/pod-product-compliance
Lightning Source LLC
LaVergne TN
LVHW061954070526
838199LV00060B/4106